WAFFLES

Tara Duggan

photographs by Erin Kunkel

weldon**owen**

CONTENTS

all about waffles

Whether they're pulled out of the toaster on a busy workday or made from scratch on a slow-moving Sunday, we tend to think of waffles only for breakfast. But waffles offer many other possibilities. From sweet to savory, from breakfast to dessert, there's room for waffles at any meal of the day.

Waffles hold a special place at the breakfast table. Anyone who has woken up on a weekend morning, padded into the kitchen, and reached to plug in a waffle iron knows the magic of the toasty aromas that fill the kitchen, tempting late risers out of bed. Waffles, because of their unique shape, seem to beg for toppings: fresh berries that nestle into the grid marks, and butter, whipped cream, and maple and fruit syrups and sauces that pool and soak into the crumb. And this is where the fun begins, because there are so many ways to top, fill, and improvise when it comes to waffles.

Think beyond breakfast, and try savory waffles laced with cheese or studded with fresh corn for a delicious dinner or appetizer. Sweet waffles made with fresh pineapple pair up with salted caramel sauce for a dramatic and seductive dessert. Waffles can even take the place of bread in inventive sandwiches, such as a grilled ham-and-cheese served with Dijon dipping sauce.

The recipes in this book are based on a handful of easy batters. A buttermilk batter works both for breakfast waffles with blackberry syrup and for dinner with chicken and gravy. But you can add all kinds of ingredients to waffle batter, including mashed potatoes for golden potato waffles with applesauce, and shredded zucchini packed into crispy waffles with nutty Asiago cheese. A cocoa-enhanced batter makes delicious chocolate waffle bites, and when topped with maple syrup and cinnamon-nutmeg whipped cream, pumpkin waffles make a delicious holiday brunch or dessert.

Mix and match batters and toppings to personalize flavors and take advantage of the ingredients you have on hand. Waffles are surprisingly easy to make. All you really need are a couple of bowls, a whisk, and a waffle maker to achieve that stack of waffles on a Sunday morning, however slow-moving. And the leftovers, which you can freeze, can take the place of weekday toaster waffles out of the box.

key ingredients

The majority of the recipes in this book call for whole milk, large eggs, and unsalted butter combined with flour and leavening, but there's lots of room for variation in flavorings and toppings.

leaveners Baking powder and baking soda cause waffles to rise. Use a double-acting baking powder, which is activated both when combined with liquid ingredients and again when subjected to heat. Baking soda is activated by the acid in buttermilk or sour cream, and helps balance those flavors.

flours and grains Unbleached all-purpose flour is the foundation of most waffle recipes. The higher the percentage of white flour, the lighter the crumb will be. But whole grains add nutrition, texture, and flavor. Whole-wheat flour is nutty in flavor, and buckwheat flour adds dark color and crispness (a traditional ingredient in Russian blini, it's a natural partner for seafood). Cornmeal also adds sweetness and crunch. Only stone-ground cornmeal is a whole grain; it requires longer cooking times than standard cornmeal. Sweet and pleasantly chewy, rolled oats are high in protein and fiber.

dairy Buttermilk adds a subtle tang to waffles, making them a good match for sweet toppings. Both sour cream and yogurt add richness and tenderness and, with added milk, can substitute for buttermilk; yogurt has the lowest fat. Fresh ricotta cheese can also be stirred directly into batters, imparting its signature light and creamy texture.

mix-ins Both fresh and still-frozen fruit can be incorporated into waffle batter or used in toppings. After adding the batter to the waffle maker, make sure the fruit is spread out evenly. Unsweetened dried coconut adds a subtle tropical flavor and chewiness. You can incorporate chocolate into waffle batters by substituting cocoa powder and sugar for some of the flour, and by adding melted chocolate along with the liquid ingredients.

maple syrup Homemade waffles deserve real maple syrup. Use pure syrup, grade A, lightly golden in color, or grade B, with more molasses flavor.

Waffle Types

The basic idea of waffles dates back to ancient history, but waffles really became popular as a street food in medieval Europe. Waffles are still served as a snack—rather than breakfast—in Belgium, where there are many regional variations. What is called a Brussels waffle is made with yeast and whipped egg whites. Liege waffles, also made with yeast, are denser, and get a distinctive caramel flavor from pearl sugar.

In the United States, a Belgian waffle refers to a waffle made with the egg whites whipped separately, as well as the style of waffle maker in which it is made. While traditional American makers turn out flat, crispy waffles, Belgian makers create deep pockets, high sides, and a more fluffy interior. All of the recipes in this book can be prepared with either type of waffle maker, but expect the yield to vary because Belgian waffle makers tend to use more batter per batch.

equipment

You won't need much more than a waffle maker and some standard measuring equipment to make waffles, and a mixer if you are preparing whipped cream. Most of today's waffle makers have nonstick plates, adjustable heat levels, and indicators that tell you when waffle maker is hot and when the waffle is done. The main decision is whether to purchase a regular or a Belgian waffle maker.

regular waffle maker Standard American waffle makers produce thin, crisp, golden waffles. You can find models that make round, square, and even heart-shaped waffles, or some that cook up to six waffles at a time. Waffle-stick makers even create single rows, perfect for dipping. Waffle makers with nonstick plates are easy to clean and make it simple to remove the finished waffles. Follow the manufacturer's instructions for preheating and greasing the unit: After plugging it in, allow several minutes for the grids to become hot. Some manufacturers say the waffle maker needs to be greased with oil or butter only the first time you use it, while others suggest greasing the plates every time you use the waffle maker, or between each batch. To clean the machine, unplug it and allow it to cool, brush away crumbs, and wipe with a clean, damp sponge and then a dry cloth.

belgian waffle maker Belgian waffle makers create waffles, both round and square, with deep, large pockets and high walls. Some make only one waffle at a time, while others make four square waffles at once, which makes cooking for a crowd easier. Some makers come with a flip mechanism that allows you to rotate the plates after adding the batter, to cook

the waffles more evenly. Again, waffle makers with nonstick plates are the most convenient choice for waffle removal and cleaning.

egg waffle pan Sweet and eggy waffles in a pattern of spheres are a popular street food in Hong Kong. At home, these can be created using a special interlocking pan with small rounded wells. Unlike electrical units, these are designed for stove top use over one or two burners.

To cook egg waffles, preheat an egg waffle pan according to the manufacturer's instructions, and brush with oil if called for. Ladle the batter into one side of the pan. Immediately place the other side of the pan on top, and flip the pan over. Cook for 2–3 minutes on the first side, flip the pan again, and continue cooking until the waffle is crisp and browned, 2–3 minutes longer. Open the pan, and invert the pan over a plate to release the waffle.

making waffles

Making waffles is easier than it may seem. Mix the dry ingredients, the wet ingredients, and possibly whip a few egg whites, and you'll be on your way.

1 preheat your waffle maker
Follow the manufacturer's instructions for preheating and greasing with oil or nonstick cooking spray, if necessary. The first waffle may be darker or lighter than the others, so experiment with the temperature at first.

2 mix the liquid ingredients
In a medium bowl, whisk together the eggs, milk, melted butter or oil, and other dairy such as sour cream and flavorings like extracts or citrus juice.

3 mix the dry ingredients
In a large bowl, mix together the flour, baking powder, baking soda, salt, and any sugar, spices, or grains. Add any cheese after the finer ingredients.

4 combine liquid and dry ingredients
Make a well in the center of the dry ingredients, then pour in the liquid ingredients.

5 don't overmix the batter
Whisk until mostly smooth, with just a few lumps. The batter should be less lumpy than a pancake batter but not overmixed or the texture of the waffles will be tough.

6 beat the egg whites (Belgian waffles)

In a stand mixer using the whisk attachment, whip the egg whites on medium-high speed until soft peaks form, 3 minutes. Add sugar, if using, and whip until firm peaks form, 2–3 minutes. With a spatula, gently fold the whites into the batter.

7 add fruit or other ingredients

Some recipes call for folding fruit and other chunky ingredients into the batter, while others add nuts to the bottom of the pan so they toast.

8 ladle the batter into the maker

Measure ½–¾ cup (4–6 fl oz/125–180 ml) batter into a measuring cup and pour it onto the grids. Use a heatproof spatula to spread the batter so that it almost reaches the edges of the waffle maker.

9 cook the waffles

Cook until the waffles are crisp and browned and steam has stopped escaping from the waffle maker. This usually takes 3–4 minutes, but you may need a few extra minutes for batters with moist ingredients such as pumpkin purée or ricotta. If the waffle isn't browned to your liking, leave it in a minute or two longer, and set a timer so you don't forget.

10 serve the waffles

Remove the waffles using a wooden or nonmetal spatula to avoid scratching nonstick surfaces. Serve your waffles right away, or keep warm, on a baking sheet in a single layer, for up to 20 minutes in a 200ºF (95ºC) oven.

waffle tips and tricks

At this point you are probably eager to get started, but there are a few more things to keep in mind to help waffle making go more smoothly. After making waffles a couple of times, you will develop an eye— and a nose—for knowing when the waffle batter is just right and when the waffles are perfectly cooked.

• Read the instruction manual to your waffle maker carefully. The manual will explain how often you should grease the plates and the best way to clean the waffle maker.

• Yields may differ depending on your type of waffle maker. A regular waffle maker tends to use less batter, and make more waffles, than a Belgian waffle maker because it makes flatter waffles. At the same time, Belgian waffles are more filling, so you won't need as many per serving.

• If you've overfilled the waffle grids, let the batter bake for a few seconds with the lid up, then slowly close the lid to finish baking the waffles. This will help keep the batter from overflowing.

• Don't open the iron until the waffles are ready. It's tempting to take a peek, but you may end up with waffles that are split down the middle. Besides the iron's indicator light, the best way to tell when the waffles are ready is when steam stops escaping.

• Butter or oil in the batter helps keep the waffles from sticking to the waffle iron. If you find that your waffles are still sticking, brush oil or melted butter onto the waffle grid before pouring in the batter, especially the first time you use it.

• Use a wooden, silicone, or rubber utensil to remove your waffles from the waffle maker. A metal fork or knife will also do the trick, but over time could damage the nonstick coating.

• Improve the crispness of waffles by placing them on a baking sheet and placing in a 300°F (150°C) oven for about 5 minutes. Always place waffles in a single layer on the pan, or on a cooling rack set on top of the pan.

• Waffles are at their best fresh out of the waffle maker, but they can be made ahead. If you are serving waffles later in the day, especially in a sandwich or with ice cream, make the waffles and place them in a single layer on a cooling rack. When they are completely cooled, stack, wrap with plastic wrap, and refrigerate. Reheat in a 300°F (150°C) oven for 5–10 minutes.

• Waffles can be frozen and reheated without thawing. Let the waffles cool completely as directed above, then place in resealable freezer bags separated by wax paper and store in the freezer. Reheat frozen waffles directly into a toaster oven or on a baking sheet in a 350°F (180°C) oven for 5–10 minutes.

• To save time in the morning, mix your ingredients the night before. Mix the dry and liquid ingredients in separate containers, and refrigerate the liquid ingredients. In the morning, stir them together in a large bowl.

waffle trivia

Waffles are delicious just stacked and drizzled with maple syrup, but you can do a whole lot more. Here are some creative ways to serve waffles beyond the standard brunch lineup:

waffle sandwiches

If you think of waffles as bread, the sandwich possibilities become endless. Fill with ham and cheese, then grill (page 65), or use toasty sourdough waffles for blockbuster BLTs (page 55).

waffles and ice cream

Serving waffles with ice cream conjures up memories of waffle cones. Vanilla Bean Belgian Waffles (page 19) are a great choice for banana splits and ice cream sandwiches.

waffle french toast

Throw your French toast in the waffle maker (page 39), and it will come out crispy and golden, especially when you add melted butter to the custard.

waffle bites

If you cut waffles into bite-size pieces, such as for Chocolate Waffle Bites with Peanut Butter Cream (page 78), they become a vehicle for all kinds of sauces; think waffle fondue.

waffle sticks

Cut three-cheese (page 66) or other waffles into strips to serve with dips, soups, or salads. You can even buy a waffle-stick maker (page 11).

chicken and waffles

Fried chicken served with waffles and gravy (page 59) is a soul food specialty that quickly becomes addictive.

BREAKFAST & BRUNCH

Belgian-style waffle recipes call for whipping the egg whites separately, which results in crisp, airy waffles. Flecked with vanilla seeds and mounded with strawberries and whipped cream, these waffles are perfect for a celebration.

Vanilla Bean Belgian Waffles with Whipped Cream and Strawberries

1½ cups (12 fl oz/375 ml) whole milk

1 vanilla bean

2 pints (1 lb/500 g) strawberries, stemmed, cored, and sliced

7 tablespoons (3½ oz/105 g) granulated sugar, divided

3 large eggs, separated

½ cup (4 oz/125 g) unsalted butter, melted

1¾ cups (9 oz/280 g) all-purpose flour

2 teaspoons baking powder

¼ teaspoon salt

Whipped Cream (page 77)

Confectioners' sugar for serving

MAKES 6–10 WAFFLES

In a small saucepan, heat the milk over medium heat until bubbles form around the edges. Remove from the heat. Split the vanilla bean in half lengthwise and use a small knife to scrape the beans into the milk. Add the vanilla pod and let stand, 30–60 minutes.

In a medium bowl, toss the strawberries and 4 tablespoons (2 oz/60 g) of the sugar. Macerate, stirring occasionally, until the berries soften and form a syrup, 30–60 minutes.

Preheat a Belgian waffle maker (see page 11).

In the bowl of a stand mixer using the whisk attachment, whip the egg whites on medium-high speed until soft peaks form, 3 minutes. Add the remaining 3 tablespoons sugar and whip until firm peaks form, 2–3 minutes. Remove the vanilla pod and place the infused milk in a medium bowl. Slowly whisk in the egg yolks and the butter.

In a large bowl, mix together the flour, baking powder, and salt. Make a well in the center of the dry ingredients, and pour in the milk mixture, stirring until just combined. Gently fold in the egg whites.

Ladle the batter into the waffle maker, using ½–¾ cup (4–6 fl oz/ 125–180 ml) batter per batch. Spread the batter so that it almost reaches the edges of the waffle maker. Cook until the waffles are crisp and browned, 3–4 minutes.

Using a spatula, remove the waffles from the waffle maker and serve right away, or place on a baking sheet in a single layer in a 200°F (95°C) oven for up to 20 minutes before serving. Top with the strawberries and whipped cream, and dust with confectioners' sugar.

These sunny-yellow waffles come out of the iron fragrant with orange zest. Sour cream, both in the batter and in the sauce, adds a tanginess that stands out against the topping of honey.

Sour Cream–Orange Waffles

For the Sour Cream–Orange Sauce

⅓ cup (2½ oz/75 g) sour cream

½ teaspoon finely grated orange zest

2 tablespoons fresh orange juice

1½ tablespoons orange blossom or other wildflower honey

2 large eggs

1 cup (8 fl oz/250 ml) whole milk

½ cup (4 oz/125 g) sour cream

½ cup (4 oz/125 g) unsalted butter, melted, or ½ cup (4 fl oz/125 ml) canola oil

2 tablespoons finely grated orange zest

2 tablespoons fresh orange juice

½ teaspoon pure vanilla extract

1½ cups (7½ oz/235 g) all-purpose flour

2 tablespoons firmly packed golden brown sugar

2 tablespoons baking powder

1 teaspoon baking soda

¼ teaspoon salt

Warm honey for serving

MAKES 4–8 WAFFLES

To make the sour cream–orange sauce, in a small bowl, mix together the sour cream, orange zest, orange juice, and honey; it will be thin.

Preheat a waffle maker (see page 11).

In a medium bowl, whisk together the eggs, milk, sour cream, butter, orange zest, orange juice, and vanilla.

In a large bowl, mix together the flour, brown sugar, baking powder, baking soda, and salt. Make a well in the center of the dry ingredients, then pour in the egg mixture. Whisk until mostly smooth, with just a few lumps.

Ladle the batter into the waffle maker, using ½–¾ cup (4–6 fl oz/ 125–180 ml) batter per batch. Spread the batter so that it almost reaches the edges of the waffle maker. Cook until the waffles are crisp and browned, 3–4 minutes.

Using a spatula, remove the waffles from the waffle maker and serve the waffles right away, or place the waffles on a baking sheet in a single layer in a 200°F (95°C) oven for up to 20 minutes before serving. Top with a spoonful of the sauce and a light drizzle of honey.

Crispy and golden, traditional buttermilk waffles are easy to mix up in the morning. The blackberry syrup features big chunks of berries in a sweet-tart sauce, or you can try Blueberry-Citrus Syrup (page 27) with these.

Classic Buttermilk Waffles with Blackberry Syrup

For the Blackberry Syrup

1 pint (8 oz/250 g) fresh or frozen blackberries

1 cinnamon stick

¼ cup (2 oz/60 g) firmly packed golden brown sugar

Buttermilk Waffle Batter (page 91)
Confectioners' sugar for serving

MAKES 4–8 WAFFLES

Egg Waffle Variation

Preheat an egg waffle pan according to the manufacturer's instructions. Ladle the batter into one side of the pan, using ¾ cup (6 fl oz/180 ml) batter per waffle. Immediately place the other side of the pan on top, and flip the pan over. Flip the pan again halfway through the cooking time (see page 11).

To make the blackberry syrup, place the blackberries, cinnamon, brown sugar, and ¼ cup (2 fl oz/60 ml) water in a small saucepan. Bring to a simmer, then reduce heat to low. Cover and gently simmer until a syrup forms but the blackberries are still in large pieces, about 10 minutes. Remove the cinnamon stick and use a spatula to scrape the contents of the saucepan into a serving pitcher. (The syrup can be made 3 days ahead. Cover tightly and refrigerate, then reheat gently to serve.)

Preheat a waffle maker (see page 11). Prepare the batter according to the directions on page 91.

Ladle the batter into the waffle maker, using ½–¾ cup (4–6 fl oz/125–180 ml) batter per batch. Spread the batter so that it almost reaches the edges of the waffle maker. Cook until the waffles are crisp and browned, 3–4 minutes.

Using a spatula, remove the waffles from the waffle maker and serve right away, or place on a baking sheet in a single layer in a 200°F (95°C) oven for up to 20 minutes before serving. Drizzle with blackberry syrup and dust with confectioners' sugar.

Gai daan jai or "little chicken eggs" is the Cantonese name for these distinctively shaped waffles. One of the most popular street foods in Hong Kong, vendors typically roll them up into a cone, for a crispy, airy treat eaten out of hand.

Hong Kong–Style Egg Waffles

Oil for greasing

2 large eggs

¾ cup (6 fl oz/180 ml) whole milk

6 tablespoons (3 oz/90 g) unsalted butter, melted

¾ cup (6 oz/185 g) granulated sugar

1 tablespoon pure vanilla extract

1 cup (5 oz/155 g) all-purpose flour

1 teaspoon baking powder

⅛ teaspoon salt

Strawberry or raspberry jam for serving

Confectioners' sugar for serving

MAKES 4 WAFFLES

Lightly oil the egg waffle pan and preheat over medium heat according to the manufacturer's instructions.

In a medium bowl, whisk together the eggs, milk, butter, granulated sugar, and vanilla.

In a large bowl, mix together the flour, baking powder, and salt. Make a well in the center of the dry ingredients, then pour in the egg mixture. Whisk until mostly smooth, with just a few lumps.

Ladle ¾ cup (6 fl oz/180 ml) batter into the center of one side of the pan. Immediately place the other side of the pan on top, flip the pan over and cook, 2–3 minutes. Flip the pan over and cook until the waffle is golden brown, 2–3 minutes longer.

Remove the pan from the heat, open the lid and invert the egg waffle onto a wire rack. Let cool for 2–3 minutes. Spread a thin layer of jam on top, dust with confectioners' sugar, then roll into a cone and serve right away.

Fragrant lemon and nutmeg, creamy ricotta cheese, and a touch of cornmeal creates waffles with a contrast of flavors and textures. The slightly tart blueberry-citrus syrup brings out the lemon flavor in the waffles.

Lemon-Ricotta Waffles with Blueberry-Citrus Syrup

For the Blueberry-Citrus Syrup

¼ cup (2 oz/60 g) firmly packed golden brown sugar

1½ cups (6 oz/185 g) fresh or frozen blueberries

6 lemon zest strips

2 large eggs, separated

1 cup (8 fl oz/250 ml) buttermilk

½ cup (4 oz/125 g) unsalted butter, melted

¾ cup (6 oz/185 g) ricotta cheese

2 tablespoons finely grated lemon zest

2 tablespoons fresh lemon juice

¼ cup (2 oz/60 g) granulated sugar

1¼ cups (6½ oz/200 g) all-purpose flour

¼ cup (1½ oz/45 g) cornmeal

2 teaspoons baking powder

¼ teaspoon salt

¼ teaspoon freshly grated nutmeg or a pinch of ground nutmeg

Confectioners' sugar for serving

MAKES 4–8 WAFFLES

To make the blueberry-citrus syrup, place ¼ cup (2 fl oz/60 ml) water and the brown sugar in a small saucepan over medium heat. Add the blueberries and lemon zest and bring to a simmer. Cook until the berries pop and form a thick syrup, about 5 minutes.

Preheat a waffle maker (see page 11).

In a medium bowl, whisk together the egg yolks, buttermilk, and butter. Gently stir in the ricotta, lemon zest, and lemon juice.

In the bowl of a stand mixer using the whisk attachment, whip the egg whites on medium-high speed until soft peaks form, about 3 minutes. Stir in the granulated sugar and whip until stiff peaks form, another 2–3 minutes.

In a large bowl, mix together the flour, cornmeal, baking powder, salt, and nutmeg. Make a well in the center of the dry ingredients, and pour in the egg mixture, stirring until just combined. Gently fold in the egg whites.

Ladle the batter into the waffle maker, using ½–¾ cup (4–6 fl oz/ 125–180 ml) batter per batch. Spread the batter so that it almost reaches the edges of the waffle maker. Cook until the waffles are crisp and browned, 4–6 minutes. These waffles tend to be slightly wet, so you have to cook them a little longer than usual.

Using a spatula, remove the waffles from the waffle maker and serve right away, or place on a baking sheet in a single layer in a 200°F (95°C) oven for up to 20 minutes before serving. Drizzle with the blueberry-citrus syrup, and dust with confectioners' sugar.

These waffles have the tart lemony flavor and seedy crunch of poppy seed cake in light, crisp waffle form. Try them with Strawberry Sauce (page 85), with maple syrup and confectioners' sugar, or on their own.

Lemon-Poppy Seed Waffles

2 large eggs

1½ cups (12 fl oz/375 ml) buttermilk

½ cup (4 oz/125 g) unsalted butter, melted

2 tablespoons finely grated lemon zest

2 tablespoons fresh lemon juice

1 teaspoon pure vanilla extract

1½ cups (7½ oz/235 g) all-purpose flour

⅓ cup (3 oz/90 g) granulated sugar

1½ teaspoons baking powder

1 teaspoon baking soda

¼ teaspoon salt

2 tablespoons poppy seeds

Strawberry Sauce (page 85) or maple syrup

Confectioners' sugar for serving

MAKES 4–8 WAFFLES

Preheat a waffle maker (see page 11).

In a medium bowl, whisk together the eggs, buttermilk, butter, lemon zest, lemon juice, and vanilla.

In a large bowl, combine the flour, granulated sugar, baking powder, baking soda, and salt. Stir in the poppy seeds. Make a well in the center of the dry ingredients, then pour in the egg mixture. Whisk until mostly smooth, with just a few lumps.

Ladle the batter into the waffle maker, using ½–¾ cup (4–6 fl oz/ 125–180 ml) batter per batch. Spread the batter so that it almost reaches the edges of the waffle maker. Cook until the waffles are crisp and browned, 3–4 minutes.

Using a spatula, remove the waffles from the waffle maker and serve right away, or place on a baking sheet in a single layer in a 200°F (95°C) oven for up to 20 minutes before serving. Top with the strawberry sauce and dust with confectioners' sugar.

Cranberry sauce makes a fresh, tangy contrast to toasty pecan-crusted waffles. You can double (or triple) the sauce to serve with roast turkey, then prepare these waffles the next day topped with the rest of the sauce.

Pecan-Crusted Waffles with Cranberry Sauce

For the Cranberry Sauce

2 cups (8 oz/250 g) fresh or frozen cranberries

½ cup (4 oz/125 g) granulated sugar, plus 2 tablespoons

2 strips orange zest

1 cinnamon stick

Buttermilk Waffle Batter (page 91)
½ cup (2 oz/60 g) pecan pieces
Confectioners' sugar for serving

MAKES 4–8 WAFFLES

To make the cranberry sauce, place the cranberries, granulated sugar, orange zest, cinnamon stick, and ½ cup (4 fl oz/125 ml) water in a saucepan. Bring the mixture to a boil over high heat, then reduce the heat to low and simmer until the sauce thickens slightly and the cranberries pop, about 10 minutes. Use a potato masher to mash the berries slightly.

Place the cranberry sauce in a serving bowl and let cool until thick, 20–30 minutes. (The cranberry sauce can be made up to 5 days ahead. Cover tightly and refrigerate, then bring to room temperature before serving.)

Preheat a waffle maker (see page 11). Prepare the batter according to the directions on page 91.

Sprinkle 2–3 tablespoons of pecans over the bottom of the waffle maker, then ladle the batter on top, using ½–¾ cup (4–6 fl oz/ 125–180 ml) batter per batch. Spread the batter so that it almost reaches the edges of the waffle maker. Cook until the waffles are crisp and browned, 3–4 minutes.

Using a spatula, remove the waffles from the waffle maker and serve, pecan side up, right away, or place on a baking sheet in a single layer in a 200°F (95°C) oven for up to 20 minutes before serving. Top with the cranberry sauce and dust with confectioners' sugar.

Ground ginger gives these waffles a hint of spiciness that complements sweet dried cranberries, which are plumped with orange juice before folding into the batter. Try them topped with Maple Butter (page 36) and dusted with sugar.

Cranberry-Ginger Waffles

1 cup (4 oz/125 g)
dried unsweetened cranberries

⅔ cup (5 fl oz/160 ml)
fresh orange juice
(from about 2 oranges)

2 large eggs

1½ cups (12 fl oz/375 ml)
whole milk

½ cup (4 oz/125 g)
unsalted butter, melted,
or ½ cup (4 fl oz/125 ml)
canola oil

1 teaspoon pure vanilla extract

1½ cups (7½ oz/235 g)
all-purpose flour

¼ cup (2 oz/60 g) firmly packed
golden brown sugar

4 teaspoons ground ginger

1 tablespoon baking powder

¼ teaspoon salt

Warm maple syrup for serving

MAKES 4-8 WAFFLES

Place the cranberries in a small bowl and toss with the orange juice. Let the cranberries soak while you prepare the batter, about 10 minutes or until softened. Drain and discard the orange juice.

Preheat a waffle maker (see page 11).

In a medium bowl, whisk together the eggs, milk, butter, and vanilla.

In a large bowl, mix together the flour, brown sugar, ginger, baking powder, and salt. Make a well in the center of the dry ingredients, then pour in the egg mixture. Whisk until mostly smooth, with just a few lumps. Gently stir in the drained cranberries.

Ladle the batter into the waffle maker, using ½–¾ cup (4–6 fl oz/ 125–180 ml) batter per batch. Spread the batter so that it almost reaches the edges of the waffle maker, and evenly distribute the cranberries. Cook until the waffles are crisp and browned, 3–4 minutes.

Using a spatula, remove the waffles from the waffle maker and serve right away, or place on a baking sheet in a single layer in a 200°F (95°C) oven for up to 20 minutes before serving. Drizzle with maple syrup.

You can hear the blueberries pop as they cook inside these nutritious waffles, which emerge with swirls of dark blue. The berries can burn easily, so start with a lower heat setting and clean the waffle maker between batches.

Whole-Wheat Blueberry Waffles

2 large eggs

1½ cups (12 fl oz/375 ml) whole milk

½ cup (4 fl oz/125 ml) canola oil

¾ cup (4 oz/125 g) all-purpose flour

¾ cup (4 oz/125 g) whole-wheat flour

2 tablespoons firmly packed golden brown sugar

1 tablespoon baking powder

½ teaspoon cinnamon

½ teaspoon salt

1 cup (4 oz/125 g) fresh or frozen blueberries

Butter for serving

Warm maple syrup for serving

MAKES 4-8 WAFFLES

Preheat a waffle maker (see page 11) to medium-low in order to avoid burning the blueberries.

In a medium bowl, whisk together the eggs, milk, and canola oil.

In a large bowl, mix together the all-purpose flour, whole-wheat flour, brown sugar, baking powder, cinnamon, and salt. Make a well in the center of the dry ingredients, then pour in the egg mixture. Whisk until mostly smooth, with just a few lumps. Gently fold in the blueberries.

Ladle the batter into the waffle maker, using ½–¾ cup (4–6 fl oz/ 125–180 ml) batter per batch. Spread the batter so that it almost reaches the edges of the waffle maker. Cook until the waffles are crisp and browned, 3–4 minutes. Wipe the waffle maker clean between batches in case there are any burned berries.

Using a spatula, remove the waffles from the waffle maker and serve right away, or place on a baking sheet in a single layer in a 200°F (95°C) oven for up to 20 minutes before serving. Top with pats of butter and drizzle with maple syrup.

There is a satisfying wholesomeness to these waffles, which are made of rolled oats and whole-wheat flour. Chunks of banana and a sprinkle of brown sugar make them great as a snack, even without maple syrup.

Oatmeal Waffles with Brown Sugar and Bananas

2 large eggs

1½ cups (12 fl oz/375 ml) whole milk

½ cup (4 oz/125 g) unsalted butter, melted, or ½ cup (4 fl oz/125 ml) canola oil

1 teaspoon pure vanilla extract

1 cup (5 oz/155 g) all-purpose flour

½ cup (2½ oz/75 g) whole-wheat flour

¾ cup (2½ oz/75 g) rolled oats

3 tablespoons firmly packed golden brown sugar, plus 2–3 tablespoons brown sugar for sprinkling

1 tablespoon baking powder

½ teaspoon cinnamon

¼ teaspoon salt

2 large ripe bananas, chopped into ¼-inch (6-mm) dice

Warm maple syrup for serving

MAKES 4–8 WAFFLES

Preheat a waffle maker (see page 11).

In a medium bowl, whisk together the eggs, milk, butter, and vanilla.

In a large bowl, combine the all-purpose flour, whole-wheat flour, oats, 3 tablespoons brown sugar, baking powder, cinnamon, and salt. Make a well in the center of the dry ingredients, then pour in the egg mixture. Whisk until mostly smooth, with just a few lumps. Gently fold in three-fourths of the bananas.

Ladle the batter into the waffle maker, using ½–¾ cup (4–6 fl oz/ 125–180 ml) batter per batch. Spread the batter so that it almost reaches the edges of the waffle maker. Sprinkle each waffle with about 1 teaspoon of brown sugar, then top with 1 or 2 pieces of banana. Cook until the waffles are crisp and browned, 3–4 minutes. Spray the waffle maker with nonstick spray between batches.

Using a spatula, remove the waffles from the waffle maker and serve right away, or place on a baking sheet in a single layer in a 200°F (95°C) oven for up to 20 minutes before serving. Serve, banana side up, drizzled with maple syrup.

Neither the waffles nor the topping in this recipe are overly sweet, highlighting the fresh, creamy flavor of the yogurt. A light drizzle of honey brings everything together. Try these topped with sliced pears or fresh figs.

Yogurt Waffles with Honey Cream

For the Honey Cream

1 cup (8 oz/250 g) plain yogurt

¼ cup (3 oz/90 g) wildflower honey

2 large eggs

1 cup (8 oz/250 g) plain yogurt

½ cup (4 fl oz/125 ml) whole milk, plus more as needed

½ cup (4 oz/125 g) unsalted butter, melted, or ½ cup (4 fl oz/125 ml) canola oil

2 tablespoons honey

1 teaspoon pure vanilla extract

1½ cups (7½ oz/235 g) all-purpose flour

1 tablespoon firmly packed golden brown sugar

2 teaspoons baking powder

1 teaspoon baking soda

¼ teaspoon salt

Warm honey for serving

MAKES 4–8 WAFFLES

To make the honey cream, in a medium bowl, whisk together the 1 cup yogurt and the honey.

Preheat a waffle maker (see page 11).

In another medium bowl, whisk together the eggs, 1 cup yogurt, milk, butter, honey, and vanilla.

In a large bowl, mix together the flour, brown sugar, baking powder, baking soda, and salt. Make a well in the center of the dry ingredients, then pour in the egg mixture. Whisk until mostly smooth, with just a few lumps. If the batter is too thick, stir in another 1–2 tablespoons milk.

Ladle the batter into the waffle maker, using ½–¾ cup (4–6 fl oz/125–180 ml) batter per batch. Spread the batter so that it almost reaches the edges of the waffle maker. Cook until the waffles are crisp and browned, 3–4 minutes.

Using a spatula, remove the waffles from the waffle maker and serve right away, or place on a baking sheet in a single layer in a 200°F (95°C) oven for up to 20 minutes before serving. Top with the honey cream and a light drizzle of honey.

Full of spices and topped with rich maple butter, these waffles are the perfect thing for holiday gatherings. Add sliced fruit and whipped cream for an extra flourish. If you are using a Belgian waffle maker, cook on medium-high.

Gingerbread Waffles with Maple Butter

For the Maple Butter

6 tablespoons (3 oz/90 g) unsalted butter, softened

1½ tablespoons pure maple syrup

Pinch of salt

Pinch of cinnamon

2 large eggs

1½ cups (12 fl oz/375 ml) whole milk

½ cup (4 oz/125 g) unsalted butter, melted, or ½ cup (4 fl oz/125 ml) canola oil

3 tablespoons dark molasses

1 teaspoon pure vanilla extract

1½ cups (7½ oz/235 g) all-purpose flour

3 tablespoons firmly packed golden brown sugar

1 tablespoon baking powder

2 teaspoons ground ginger

1 teaspoon cinnamon

¼ teaspoon ground cloves

½ teaspoon salt

Warm maple syrup for serving (optional)

MAKES 4–8 WAFFLES

To make the maple butter, in a small bowl, whisk together the butter, maple syrup, salt, and cinnamon. Scoop into a ramekin or other serving dish. Place in the freezer for 5 minutes or in the refrigerator for 15 minutes to firm up before serving.

Preheat a waffle maker (see page 11).

In a medium bowl, whisk together the eggs, milk, butter, molasses, and vanilla.

In a large bowl, mix together the flour, brown sugar, baking powder, ginger, cinnamon, cloves, and salt. Make a well in the center of the dry ingredients, then pour in the egg mixture. Whisk until mostly smooth, with just a few lumps.

Ladle the batter into the waffle maker, using ½–¾ cup (4–6 fl oz/ 125–180 ml) batter per batch. Spread the batter so that it almost reaches the edges of the waffle maker. Cook until the waffles are crisp and browned, 3–4 minutes.

Using a spatula, remove the waffles from the waffle maker and serve right away, or place on a baking sheet in a single layer in a 200°F (95°C) oven for up to 20 minutes before serving. Top with pats of maple butter and drizzle with maple syrup, if using.

Why not put your French toast in the waffle iron? It comes out extra crispy, with a golden-brown pattern. Instead of maple syrup, try this with Blueberry-Citrus Syrup (page 27), Blackberry Syrup (page 23), or Strawberry Sauce (page 85).

Waffled French Toast

3 large eggs

1½ cups (12 fl oz/375 ml) whole milk

2 tablespoons unsalted butter, melted, or canola oil

1 teaspoon pure vanilla extract

½ teaspoon ground cinnamon

Pinch of salt

1 lb (500 g) white egg bread, such as challah or Hawaiian bread, preferably day-old (see Note)

Butter for serving

Warm maple syrup for serving

MAKES 4 SERVINGS

Preheat a waffle maker (see page 11).

In a 9-by-13-inch (23-by-33-cm) baking dish, whisk together the eggs, milk, butter, vanilla, cinnamon, and salt.

Cut the bread evenly into ½-inch (12-mm) slices that will fit the length of your waffle iron. If you are using a round waffle maker, cut a few pieces of varying lengths. Dip each piece of bread in the egg mixture, letting it stand until it is saturated but not so soft that it falls apart, about 30 seconds per side. Place 2 pieces of bread or enough to fit in the waffle iron, close the lid, and cook until crisp and browned, 3–4 minutes. (You may need to cook the French toast longer than the waffle iron indicates.)

Using a spatula, remove the French toast from the waffle maker and serve right away, or place on a baking sheet in a single layer in a 200°F (95°C) oven for up to 20 minutes before serving. Top with pats of butter and drizzle with maple syrup.

NOTE: Dry bread soaks up the batter better than fresh bread and its lack of moisture helps prevent the pieces from falling apart when they are soaked. You can slice fresh bread, spread it out on baking sheets, and leave it at room temperature overnight to dry out.

Warm pumpkin waffles with pillows of spiced cream and drizzles of maple syrup deliver the flavors of autumn. Freshly grated nutmeg imparts the best flavor, but you can substitute ground, using half the amount.

Pumpkin Waffles with Cinnamon-Nutmeg Cream

For the Cinnamon-Nutmeg Cream

1 cup (8 fl oz/250 ml) heavy cream

3 tablespoons granulated sugar

1½ teaspoons ground cinnamon

¾ teaspoon freshly grated nutmeg

½ teaspoon pure vanilla extract

2 large eggs

1 cup (8 fl oz/250 ml) whole milk

1 cup (8 oz/250 g) canned pumpkin purée

½ cup (4 oz/125 g) unsalted butter, melted, or ½ cup (4 fl oz/125 ml) canola oil

1 teaspoon pure vanilla extract

1½ cups (7½ oz/235 g) all-purpose flour

3 tablespoons firmly packed golden brown sugar

1 tablespoon baking powder

1 teaspoon each ground ginger and ground cinnamon

½ teaspoon salt

¼ teaspoon freshly grated nutmeg

Warm maple syrup for serving

MAKES 4–8 WAFFLES

To make the cinnamon-nutmeg cream, in the bowl of a stand mixer using the whisk attachment, whip the cream on medium-high speed until soft peaks form, about 3 minutes. Add the sugar, cinnamon, nutmeg, and vanilla, and whisk until just set, 1–2 minutes. (The cream can be made 3 hours ahead; cover and refrigerate.)

Preheat a waffle maker (see page 11).

In a medium bowl, whisk together the eggs, milk, pumpkin, butter, and vanilla.

In a large bowl, mix together the flour, brown sugar, baking powder, ginger, cinnamon, salt, and nutmeg. Make a well in the center of the dry ingredients, then pour in the egg mixture. Whisk until mostly smooth, with just a few lumps.

Ladle the batter into the waffle maker, using ½–¾ cup (4–6 fl oz/ 125–180 ml) batter per batch. Spread the batter so that it almost reaches the edges of the waffle maker. Cook until the waffles are crisp and browned, 3–4 minutes.

Using a spatula, remove the waffles from the waffle maker and serve right away, or place on a baking sheet in a single layer in a 200°F (95°C) oven for up to 20 minutes before serving. Top with the cinnamon-nutmeg cream and drizzle with maple syrup.

Buckwheat flour makes nutritious, crunchy, and nutty waffles. While savory toppings like smoked salmon, dill sour cream, and capers take them out of the ordinary, these waffles are also delicious with sliced fresh fruit and maple syrup.

Buckwheat Waffles with Smoked Salmon, Dill Sour Cream, and Capers

For the Dill Sour Cream

½ cup (4 oz/125 g) sour cream

2 tablespoons chopped fresh dill

1 tablespoon finely chopped shallots or green onions

2 large eggs

2 cups (16 fl oz/500 ml) buttermilk, plus more as needed

½ cup (4 oz/125 g) unsalted butter, melted

¾ cup (4 oz/125 g) all-purpose flour

¾ cup (4 oz/125 g) buckwheat flour

2 teaspoons sugar

2 teaspoons baking powder

1½ teaspoons baking soda

½ teaspoon salt

2 large ripe tomatoes, thinly sliced (optional)

8 oz (250 g) thinly sliced smoked salmon or gravlax

¼ cup (2 oz/60 g) capers

MAKES 4–8 WAFFLES

To make the dill sour cream, in a small bowl, mix together the sour cream, dill, and shallots.

Preheat a waffle maker (see page 11).

In a medium bowl, whisk together the eggs, buttermilk, and butter.

In a large bowl, mix together the all-purpose flour, buckwheat flour, sugar, baking powder, baking soda, and salt. Make a well in the center of the dry ingredients and pour in the egg mixture. Whisk until mostly smooth, with just a few lumps.

Ladle the batter into the waffle maker, using ½–¾ cup (4–6 fl oz/ 125–180 ml) batter per batch. Spread the batter so that it almost reaches the edges of the waffle maker. Cook until the waffles are crisp and browned, 3–4 minutes.

Using a spatula, remove the waffles from the waffle maker and serve right away, or place on a baking sheet in a single layer in a 200°F (95°C) oven for up to 20 minutes before serving. Top each waffle with 1 tomato slice, if using, 1–2 slices of salmon, a dollop of dill sour cream, and a scattering of capers.

Cornmeal waffles dotted with smoky bacon bits are reminiscent of cornbread hot out of the oven. Top them with slightly savory maple syrup perfumed with fresh thyme and black peppercorns, and you may get requests for extras.

Cornmeal-Bacon Waffles with Thyme-Infused Syrup

For the Thyme-Infused Syrup

4 small sprigs fresh thyme

½ cup (5½ oz/170 g) maple syrup

5 black peppercorns

1 lb (500 g) thick-cut bacon

Cornmeal Waffle Batter (page 92), made with optional black pepper

MAKES 4–8 WAFFLES

Egg Waffle Variation

Preheat an egg waffle pan according to the manufacturer's instructions. Ladle the batter into one side of the pan, using ¾ cup (6 fl oz/180 ml) batter per waffle. Immediately place the other side of the pan on top, and flip the pan over. Flip the pan again halfway through the cooking time (see page 11).

To make the thyme-infused syrup, pull off most of the leaves from the thyme and place them and the stems in a small saucepan with the maple syrup, peppercorns, and 2 tablespoons water. Simmer over very low heat to infuse the thyme flavor into the syrup, about 10 minutes. Strain into a serving pitcher. (You can make the syrup up to 3 days ahead. Cover tightly and refrigerate; reheat gently to serve.)

Heat a heavy frying pan or griddle over medium heat and add the bacon. Cook until crisp, turning once, 7–10 minutes. Drain on paper towels, then crumble into small pieces when cool enough to handle. You should have about 1¼ cups (7½ oz/235 g).

Preheat a waffle maker (see page 11). Make the batter according to the directions on page 92, then gently fold in the bacon.

Ladle the batter into the waffle maker, using ½–¾ cup (4–6 fl oz/ 125–180 ml) batter per batch. Spread the batter so that it almost reaches the edges of the waffle maker. Cook until the waffles are crisp and browned, 3–4 minutes.

Using a spatula, remove the waffles from the waffle maker and serve right away, or place on a baking sheet in a single layer in a 200°F (95°C) oven for 20 minutes before serving. Drizzle with the thyme-infused syrup.

LUNCH & DINNER

Peanut butter waffles with warm jam and a smear of extra peanut butter make for gooey, luscious sandwiches you can eat with a fork and knife. Or, you can use your hands if you don't mind getting a little messy.

PB&J Waffle Sandwiches

1 cup (10 oz/315 g) jam or preserves of your choice, such as raspberry, strawberry, or blackberry

2 large eggs

1½ cups (12 fl oz/375 ml) whole milk

½ cup (5 oz/155 g) creamy natural peanut butter, plus about ½ cup (5 oz/155 g) for the sandwiches (see Note)

¼ cup (2 oz/60 g) unsalted butter, melted, or ¼ cup (2 fl oz/60 ml) canola oil

1½ cups (7½ oz/235 g) all-purpose flour

3 tablespoons sugar

1 tablespoon baking powder

½ teaspoon salt

MAKES 4–8 WAFFLES

Place the jam in a small microwave-safe bowl or a small saucepan. Heat until just gently warmed and loose enough to pour, 30 seconds in the microwave or about 3 minutes on the stove top over low heat, stirring. Stir and place in a serving bowl or pitcher.

Preheat a waffle maker (see page 11).

In the bowl of a stand mixer using the paddle attachment, whip the eggs, milk, ½ cup peanut butter, and butter on medium speed until smooth, 2 minutes.

In a medium bowl, mix together the flour, sugar, baking powder, and salt. With the mixer on low speed, add the dry ingredients to the peanut butter mixture until just combined.

Ladle the batter into the waffle maker, using ½–¾ cup (4–6 fl oz/ 125–180 ml) batter per batch. Spread the batter so that it almost reaches the edges of the waffle maker. Cook until the waffles are crisp and browned, 3–4 minutes.

Using a spatula, remove the waffles from the waffle maker. Cut regular waffles in half, or separate large Belgian waffles into quarters. Place a waffle piece on a plate, and spread some peanut butter on top. Pour some of the warmed jam on top, then top with another piece of waffle, or leave open-faced if using thicker Belgian waffles. Repeat with the remaining waffles and serve right away.

NOTE: For best results, use salted but unsweetened peanut butter.

The summertime flavors of sweet corn and roasted red bell peppers only get better paired with tart, creamy goat cheese in these savory waffles. Think of the waffles as a quiche, and serve topped with salad or alongside soup.

Fresh Corn, Goat Cheese, and Roasted Pepper Waffles

1 large ear fresh corn, shucked

2 large eggs

1½ cups (12 fl oz/375 ml) buttermilk

½ cup (4 fl oz/125 ml) extra-virgin olive oil or canola oil

1¼ cups (6½ oz/200 g) all-purpose flour

¼ cup (1½ oz/45 g) cornmeal

2 tablespoons sugar

2 teaspoons baking powder

1 teaspoon baking soda

½ teaspoon salt

¼ teaspoon freshly ground pepper

4 red bell peppers, roasted, peeled, seeded, and chopped (about ¾ cup)

3 oz (90 g) crumbled fresh goat cheese, plus more for serving (optional)

MAKES 5–10 WAFFLES

Prepare a steamer, and steam the corn until tender, about 5 minutes. Set aside until cool enough to handle, then remove the corn from the cob with a large knife. Break up the kernels and put in a small bowl. Using the flat end of the knife, scrape the cob over the bowl to get the "milk" and smaller pieces of corn to fall into the bowl.

Preheat a waffle maker (see page 11).

In a medium bowl, whisk together the eggs, buttermilk, and olive oil. In a large bowl, mix together the flour, cornmeal, sugar, baking powder, baking soda, salt, and pepper. Make a well in the center of the dry ingredients and pour in the liquid mixture. Whisk until mostly smooth, with just a few lumps. Fold in the corn, bell peppers, and 3 oz (90 g) goat cheese.

Ladle the batter into the waffle maker, using ½–¾ cup (4–6 fl oz/ 125–180 ml) batter per batch. Spread the batter so that it almost reaches the edges of the waffle maker. Cook until the waffles are crisp and browned, 4–5 minutes.

Using a spatula, remove the waffles from the waffle maker and serve right away, or place on a baking sheet in a single layer in a 200°F (95°C) oven for up to 20 minutes before serving. Top with extra goat cheese, if using.

With ribbons of spinach, crunchy pine nuts, fluffy ricotta, and a hint of Parmesan, these waffles are not only full of flavor but pretty, too. Serve with Tomato Chutney (page 56) or as a base for eggs Benedict.

Spinach and Ricotta Waffles with Pine Nuts

2 large eggs

1 cup (8 fl oz/250 ml) whole milk

½ cup (4 oz/125 g) unsalted butter, melted, or ½ cup (4 fl oz/125 ml) canola oil

1 cup (8 oz/250 g) ricotta cheese

1¼ cups (6½ oz/200 g) all-purpose flour

¼ cup (1½ oz/45 g) cornmeal

1 tablespoon baking powder

¾ teaspoon salt

1½ cups (4 oz/125 g) frozen chopped spinach, thawed and squeezed dry (see Note)

¼ cup (1 oz/30 g) shredded Parmesan cheese

½ cup (2½ oz/75 g) pine nuts

MAKES 4–8 WAFFLES

Preheat a waffle maker (see page 11) to medium-low.

In a medium bowl, whisk together the eggs, milk, and butter. Stir in the ricotta until smooth.

In a large bowl, mix together the flour, cornmeal, baking powder, and salt. Make a well in the center of the dry ingredients and pour in the egg mixture, stirring until just combined. Gently fold in the spinach and Parmesan cheese.

Sprinkle 1–2 tablespoons pine nuts into the waffle maker (use 2 tablespoons for large Belgian-style waffles), then ladle in the batter, using ½–¾ cup (4–6 fl oz/125–180 ml) batter per batch. Spread the batter so that it almost reaches the edges of the waffle maker. Cook until the waffles are crisp and browned, 4–6 minutes. These waffles tend to be slightly wet, so cook them a little longer than usual.

Using a spatula, remove the waffles from the waffle maker and serve right away, or place on a baking sheet in a single layer in a 200°F (95°C) oven for up to 20 minutes before serving.

NOTE: To squeeze spinach dry, place thawed spinach in a colander and squeeze handfuls at a time until almost all of the liquid is gone.

It's hard to think of a better way to use up a summertime bounty of zucchini than in these savory waffles. Though packed with summer squash, they come out light and crispy. Serve as is or with sausages and a salad.

Zucchini-Asiago Waffles

1 lb (500 g) zucchini, shredded on the large holes of a box shredder

1¾ cups (9 oz/280 g) all-purpose flour, divided

2 large eggs

1½ cups (12 fl oz/375 ml) buttermilk

½ cup (4 fl oz/125 ml) extra-virgin olive oil or canola oil

2 tablespoons sugar

2 teaspoons baking powder

1 teaspoon baking soda

1 teaspoon salt

½ teaspoon freshly ground black pepper

1 cup (4 oz/125 g) grated Asiago cheese

1 teaspoon minced fresh thyme (optional)

MAKES 6-10 WAFFLES

Place the shredded zucchini in a medium bowl and toss well with ½ cup (2½ oz/75 g) of the flour. Let stand while you prepare the rest of the batter. This absorbs some of the moisture from the zucchini.

Preheat a waffle maker (see page 11) to medium-high.

In a medium bowl, whisk together the eggs, buttermilk, and olive oil.

In a large bowl, mix the remaining 1¼ cups (6½ oz/200 g) flour, the sugar, baking powder, baking soda, salt, and pepper. Make a well in the center of the dry ingredients and pour in the liquid mixture. Whisk until mostly smooth, with just a few lumps. Gently fold in the zucchini and Asiago, and the thyme, if using.

Ladle the batter into the waffle maker, using ½-¾ cup (4-6 fl oz/ 125-180 ml) batter per batch. Spread the batter so that it almost reaches the edges of the waffle maker. Cook until the waffles are crisp and browned and you don't see steam releasing, about 3-4 minutes. Test a waffle and make sure it's not too wet in the middle; if it is, adjust the heat on the waffle maker or cook the waffles a little longer.

Using a spatula, remove the waffles from the waffle maker and serve right away, or place on a baking sheet in a single layer in a 200°F (95°C) oven for up to 20 minutes before serving.

If you make the Overnight Sourdough Waffles (page 93) for breakfast, you can use any leftover batter—which holds for three days in the refrigerator—in these incredible sandwiches. Make sure the waffles are crisp for the best results.

Sourdough Waffle BLTs

8 slices thick-cut bacon

About ½ recipe Overnight Sourdough Waffle Batter (page 93), to make 4 waffles

3 tablespoons mayonnaise

8 slices from 2 ripe tomatoes

Lettuce leaves or baby arugula

Salt and freshly ground pepper

MAKES 4 SANDWICHES

Preheat a waffle maker (see page 11). Preheat the oven to 200°F (95°C). Set a large cooling rack on top of a baking sheet.

Heat a heavy frying pan or griddle over medium heat and add the bacon. Cook until crisp, turning once, 7–10 minutes. Drain the bacon on paper towels.

Prepare the batter according to the directions on page 93. Ladle the batter into the waffle maker, using ½–¾ cup (4–6 fl oz/125–180 ml) batter per batch. Spread the batter so that it almost reaches the edges of the waffle maker. Cook until the waffles are crisp and browned, 3–4 minutes.

Using a spatula, remove the waffles from the waffle maker and place on the prepared baking sheet in a single layer in the oven until all of the waffles are cooked.

Cut the waffles in half, and spread both sides lightly with mayonnaise. Top 4 halves each with 2 pieces of the bacon, 2 slices of the tomato, and enough lettuce to cover. Season lightly with salt and pepper and top with the other waffle half. Serve right away.

Cornmeal waffles can go in a sweet or savory direction, and here they match up with a tangy, spicy sauce. Ripe cherry tomatoes make a slightly sweet, intense chutney that pairs beautifully with the corn flavor in the batter.

Cornmeal Waffles with Tomato Chutney

For the Tomato Chutney

2 tablespoons canola oil

1 cup (5 oz/155 g) finely diced onion

1 clove garlic, minced

1 teaspoon *each* brown mustard seeds and ground ginger

½ fresh jalapeño chile, minced

3 cups (18 oz/560 g) cherry tomatoes

¼ cup (2 fl oz/60 ml) cider vinegar

2 tablespoons brown sugar

1 stick cinnamon

Salt

Cornmeal Waffle Batter (page 92)

MAKES 4–8 SERVINGS

Egg Waffle Variation

Preheat an egg waffle pan according to the manufacturer's instructions. Ladle the batter into one side of the pan, using ¾ cup (6 fl oz/180 ml) batter per waffle. Immediately place the other side of the pan on top, and flip the pan over. Flip the pan again halfway through the cooking time (see page 11).

To make the tomato chutney, in a frying pan over medium-low heat, warm the oil. Add the onion, garlic, mustard seeds, ginger, and chile, and cook, stirring often, until the onions are tender, about 5 minutes. Add the tomatoes, cover, and cook, stirring occasionally, until the tomatoes start to collapse, about 5 minutes. Add the vinegar and scrape any brown bits on the bottom of the pan. If the pan is dry, add up to ¼ cup (2 fl oz/60 ml) water. Add the brown sugar and cinnamon.

Bring to a simmer and cook until the flavors come together and the tomatoes form a chunky sauce, about 10 minutes. Season to taste with salt and keep at room temperature. (The chutney can be made up to 3 days ahead, covered tightly in the refrigerator. Reheat gently or bring to room temperature before serving.)

Preheat a waffle maker (see page 11). Prepare the batter according to the directions on page 92.

Ladle the batter into the waffle maker, using ½–¾ cup (4–6 fl oz/ 125–180 ml) batter per batch. Spread the batter so that it almost reaches the edges of the waffle maker. Cook until the waffles are crisp and browned, 3–4 minutes.

Using a spatula, remove the waffles from the waffle maker and serve right away, or place on a baking sheet in a single layer in a 200°F (95°C) oven for up to 20 minutes before serving. Top with the tomato chutney.

Waffles topped with crispy chicken and smothered in gravy are a tempting soul food specialty. Those who prefer eating their waffles with syrup, and the chicken on the side, will love Thyme-Infused Syrup (page 44) here.

Chicken and Waffles with Pan Gravy

4 lb (2 kg) chicken pieces

1 cup (8 fl oz/250 ml) buttermilk or whole milk

2 large eggs

2 cups (3 oz/90 g) panko bread crumbs

1 cup (5 oz/155 g) all-purpose flour

4 teaspoons salt

2 teaspoons paprika

2 teaspoons dried thyme leaves

1 teaspoon freshly ground pepper

½–1 cup (4–8 fl oz/125–250 ml) canola oil

(continued on page 60)

MAKES 4–8 WAFFLES

To make the chicken, preheat the oven to 400°F (200°C).

Remove any excess skin and fat from the chicken, and separate the legs, thighs, breasts, and wings. If desired, cut the breasts in half.

In a large bowl, whisk together the buttermilk and eggs. Add the chicken pieces and turn to coat. Place the bread crumbs, flour, salt, paprika, thyme, and pepper in a shallow baking pan and mix thoroughly. Working with 1 piece of chicken at a time, let the excess buttermilk mixture drip off the chicken, then dredge in the bread crumb mixture. Place the coated chicken pieces on a baking sheet.

In each of 1 or 2 Dutch ovens or large heavy frying pans, add ¼ cup (2 fl oz/60 ml) of the oil or enough to coat the bottom of the pan generously. Heat the oil over medium heat until hot but not smoking. Add the chicken in batches and fry until browned, 2–3 minutes per side (it will brown more in the oven). If you notice the chicken burning, move the pieces and reduce the heat slightly. Repeat with the remaining chicken and oil, placing the finished pieces on a large rimmed baking sheet or two 9-by-13-inch (23-by-33-cm) baking pans, with space between each piece. Reserve the contents of the frying pan. (You can brown the chicken 4 hours ahead. Let cool at room temperature, then drape with plastic wrap and refrigerate.)

Place the chicken in the oven and roast until the juices run clear or a thermometer inserted into the thickest part of a piece reads 165°F (74°C), 40–60 minutes.

(Recipe continued on page 60)

Pan Gravy

1 cup (5 oz/155 g)
finely chopped onion

2 tablespoons unsalted butter

¼ cup (1½ oz/45 g)
all-purpose flour

3 cups (24 fl oz/750 ml)
reduced-sodium chicken broth

¼ cup (2 fl oz/60 ml)
heavy cream (optional)

Salt and freshly ground pepper

Buttermilk Waffle Batter (page 91)
or Cornmeal Waffle Batter
(page 92)

(Recipe continued from page 59)

To make the pan gravy, drain all but 2 tablespoons of the fat from the frying pan. Leave in any stray crispy bits. Place the pan over medium-low heat and cook the onion, stirring often, until softened, about 8 minutes. Add the butter, and when it has melted, whisk in the flour. Whisking constantly, cook until a light brown roux forms, about 4 minutes. Whisk in the broth, then bring to a simmer. Cook at a steady simmer until thickened, about 15 minutes. Stir in the cream, if using, and simmer gently, another 2 minutes. Season generously with salt and pepper and place in a warmed gravy boat.

To make the waffles, preheat a waffle maker (see page 11). Prepare the buttermilk or the cornmeal waffle batter according to the directions on page 91 or 92.

Ladle the batter into the waffle maker, using ½–¾ cup (4–6 fl oz/ 125–180 ml) batter per batch. Spread the batter so that it almost reaches the edges of the waffle maker. Cook until the waffles are crisp and browned, 3–4 minutes.

Using a spatula, remove the waffles from the waffle maker and serve right away, or place on a baking sheet in a single layer in a 200°F (95°C) oven for up to 20 minutes before serving. Top with a piece of chicken and pass the gravy alongside.

Savory sun-dried tomato pesto and creamy avocado slices turn wholesome multigrain waffles into a satisfying lunch or dinner. If you have leftover pesto, serve it over pasta with a grating of Parmesan cheese.

Multigrain Waffles with Avocado and Tomato-Almond Pesto

For the Tomato-Almond Pesto

1 cup (3 oz/90 g) dry-packed sun-dried tomatoes

1 cup (8 fl oz/250 ml) boiling water

2 garlic cloves, trimmed

½ cup (2½ oz/75 g) whole almonds

½ cup (½ oz/15 g) fresh basil leaves

¼ cup (1 oz/30 g) freshly grated Parmesan

1 cup (8 fl oz/250 ml) extra-virgin olive oil

Salt and freshly ground pepper

Multigrain Waffle Batter (page 92)

2–3 ripe avocadoes, pitted, peeled, and sliced

MAKES 4–8 WAFFLES

To make the tomato-almond pesto, place the sun-dried tomatoes in a small bowl and cover with boiling water to soften for 10 minutes. Drain, reserving the water.

Place the garlic in a blender and pulse until chopped. Add the almonds and pulse just until evenly chopped. Add the tomatoes, basil, and Parmesan, and process until blended but still a bit chunky. With the blender running, add the oil in a steady stream. The pesto should be quite thick at this point; add up to ½ cup (4 fl oz/125 ml) of the reserved soaking water to loosen it, then add salt and pepper to taste. (The pesto keeps for up to a week; cover tightly and refrigerate, then bring to room temperature before serving.)

Preheat a waffle maker (see page 11). Prepare the batter according to the directions on page 92.

Ladle the batter into the waffle maker, using ½–¾ cup (4–6 fl oz/125–180 ml) batter per batch. Spread the batter so that it almost reaches the edges of the waffle maker. Cook until the waffles are crisp and browned, 3–4 minutes.

Using a spatula, remove the waffles from the waffle maker and serve right away, or place on a baking sheet in a single layer in a 200°F (95°C) oven for up to 20 minutes before serving. To serve, spread the waffles with 2–4 tablespoons of the pesto, depending on the size of the waffle, and place avocado slices on top. Season the avocado slices lightly with salt.

Small crispy bites of waffles become an appetizer or snack when
served with a piquant red pepper sauce. Adding puréed bell peppers
to the aioli creates a thin sauce that is perfect for dipping.

Waffle Bites with Roasted Pepper Aioli

For the Roasted Pepper Aioli

**2 red bell peppers, roasted and
peeled (drained if from a jar)**

1 clove garlic, trimmed

1 large egg

2 teaspoons fresh lemon juice

½ teaspoon salt

**1 cup (8 fl oz/250 ml) olive oil
(or use half canola oil and
half olive oil)**

**Buttermilk Waffle Batter (page 91)
or Cornmeal Waffle Batter
(page 92)**

MAKES 6-8 SERVINGS

Egg Waffle Variation

Preheat an egg waffle pan
according to the manufacturer's
instructions. Ladle the batter
into one side of the pan, using
¾ cup (6 fl oz/180 ml) batter per
waffle. Immediately place the
other side of the pan on top,
and flip the pan over. Flip the
pan again halfway through
the cooking time (see page 11).

To make the roasted pepper aioli, place the bell peppers in a blender
or food processor and pulse until finely chopped. Scrape into a small
bowl and set aside. Add the garlic to the blender and pulse until
chopped. Add the egg, lemon juice, and salt, and purée until frothy,
about 2 minutes.

With the blender or food processor running, add a few drops of the
olive oil. Continue adding a little more at a time until an emulsion
starts to form, then begin adding the rest of the oil in a steady
stream. When you have added about half of the oil, you should notice
the sauce starting to thicken. Add the bell pepper purée and adjust
the seasoning with more salt or lemon juice, if you like. Chill for at
least 1 hour to overnight before serving.

Preheat a waffle maker (see page 11). Prepare the buttermilk or
cornmeal waffle batter according to the directions on page 91 or 92.

Ladle the batter into the waffle maker, using ½–¾ cup (4–6 fl oz/
125–180 ml) batter per batch. Spread the batter so that it almost
reaches the edges of the waffle maker. Cook until the waffles are
crisp and browned, 3–4 minutes.

Using a spatula, remove the waffles from the waffle maker. Cut
them into 1-inch (2.5-cm) strips, then to make bite-sized pieces.
Serve right away, or place the waffles on a baking sheet in a single
layer in a 200°F (95°C) oven for up to 20 minutes before serving.
Serve with the roasted pepper aioli.

Grilled sandwiches taste fabulous when you use waffles as the bread. Serve whole sandwiches for lunch, or slice them into wedges for appetizers. You can cook these either in the oven or on the stove top.

Ham and Cheddar Waffle Sandwiches with Dijon Dipping Sauce

For the Dijon Dipping Sauce

½ cup (4 oz/125 g) sour cream

3 tablespoons Dijon mustard

1 tablespoon whole milk or buttermilk

¼ teaspoon freshly ground pepper

1–2 teaspoons chopped fresh chives or flat-leaf parsley (optional)

2 cooked regular waffles (see Note), split into 8 quarters

2 tablespoons unsalted butter, softened

1–1¼ cups (4–5 oz/125–155 g) shredded Cheddar cheese

6–8 oz (185–250 g) thinly sliced ham

MAKES 4 SERVINGS

If cooking the sandwiches in the oven, preheat it to 400°F (200°C). Line a baking sheet with foil.

To make the Dijon dipping sauce, in a bowl, mix together the sour cream, Dijon mustard, milk, pepper, and chives, if using. Place the sauce in ramekins for dipping.

Spread the waffle pieces liberally with butter on one side. Top half of the pieces, buttered side down, with some of the cheese, then the ham, and then more cheese. Form a sandwich by placing the remaining waffle pieces, buttered side up, on top. (Having cheese on both sides of the ham helps hold the sandwich together.)

If using the oven, place the sandwiches on the prepared baking sheet and bake until the waffles are crisp on the outside and the cheese has melted, about 10 minutes. If using the stove top, preheat a heavy cast-iron frying pan or griddle over medium-low to medium heat. Add the sandwiches to the pan and cook until the cheese melts and the sandwiches brown, 4–5 minutes per side. Watch carefully, as the waffles burn easily.

Cut the sandwiches in half and serve right away with the Dijon dipping sauce.

NOTE: Buckwheat Waffles (page 43), Buttermilk Waffle Batter (page 91), and Cornmeal Waffle Batter (page 92) are all good choices here. If you are using leftover, frozen waffles (page 14), don't toast them first or they might burn. Let them thaw slightly for a few minutes at room temperature before spreading with butter.

Waffle-stick makers produce thin crispy bites, but you can also use your regular waffle maker and cut the finished waffles into strips for appetizers. These are delicious dipped in Roasted Pepper Aioli (page 62), or served with tomato soup.

Three-Cheese Waffle Sticks

2 large eggs, separated

1½ cups (12 fl oz/375 ml) buttermilk

⅓ cup (3 oz/90 g) unsalted butter, melted, or ⅓ cup (3 fl oz/80 ml) olive oil or canola oil

1¾ cups (9 oz/280 g) all-purpose flour

¼ cup (1½ oz/45 g) cornmeal

2 teaspoons baking powder

1 teaspoon baking soda

½ teaspoon salt

¼ teaspoon freshly ground black pepper

½ cup (2 oz/60 g) shredded Parmesan cheese

½ cup (2 oz/60 g) shredded creamy melting cheese, such as mozzarella or fontina

½ cup (2½ oz/75 g) finely crumbled feta or fresh goat cheese

MAKES 6-8 SERVINGS

Preheat a waffle-stick maker or regular waffle maker (see page 11).

In a medium bowl, whisk together the egg yolks, buttermilk, and butter. In a large bowl, mix together the flour, cornmeal, baking powder, baking soda, salt, and pepper.

Using a stand mixer fitted with the whisk attachment, whip the egg whites on medium-high speed until firm peaks form, 5–6 minutes.

Make a well in the center of the dry ingredients and pour in the buttermilk mixture, stirring until just combined. Gently fold in the egg whites, then fold in the three cheeses.

Ladle the batter into the waffle maker, using ½–¾ cup (4–6 fl oz/ 125–180 ml) batter per batch if using a waffle maker. Spread the batter so that it almost reaches the edges of the waffle maker. Cook until the waffles are crisp and browned, 3–4 minutes. (If using a waffle-stick maker, follow the manufacturer's instructions.)

Using a spatula, remove the waffles from the waffle or waffle-stick maker. Cut whole waffles into quarters, then slice into sticks about 1 inch (2.5 cm) wide. Serve right away, or place the waffle sticks on a baking sheet in a single layer in a 200°F (95°C) oven for up to 20 minutes before serving.

These savory golden waffles turn out best when made in a regular flat waffle iron, which can render the potatoes extra crispy. These waffles are also delicious served with fried eggs; in that case, skip the applesauce.

Potato Waffles with Applesauce

8 oz (250 g) russet or large waxy potatoes (for 1 cup mashed potatoes; see Note)

1 teaspoon salt

2 large eggs

2 cups (16 fl oz/500 ml) buttermilk

½ cup (4 oz/125 g) unsalted butter, melted, or ½ cup (4 fl oz/125 ml) canola oil

1½ cups (7½ oz/235 g) all-purpose flour

2 teaspoons baking powder

1 teaspoon baking soda

¼ teaspoon freshly ground pepper

1 cup (9 oz/280 g) lightly sweetened applesauce, at room temperature

Sour cream for serving

MAKES 6–10 WAFFLES

Place the potatoes in a saucepan covered with water by 4 inches (10 cm). Season the water with ½ teaspoon salt, bring to a boil, and then reduce the heat to a simmer and cook until the potatoes are tender when pierced with a knife, 25–30 minutes. When cool enough to handle, peel and mash the potatoes or run them through a ricer or a food mill. Let cool. (You can cook and mash the potatoes 1 day ahead. Cover and refrigerate.)

Preheat a waffle maker (see page 11).

In a medium bowl, whisk together the eggs, buttermilk, and butter. Gently mix in the potatoes.

In a large bowl, mix together the flour, baking powder, baking soda, remaining ½ teaspoon salt, and the pepper. Make a well in the center of the dry ingredients, then pour in the egg mixture. Whisk until mostly smooth, with just a few lumps.

Ladle the batter into the waffle maker, using ½–¾ cup (4–6 fl oz/ 125–180 ml) batter per batch. Spread the batter so that it almost reaches the edges of the waffle maker. Cook until the waffles are crisp and browned, 3–4 minutes.

Using a spatula, remove the waffles from the waffle maker and serve right away with the applesauce and sour cream.

NOTE: You can easily use leftover mashed potatoes here; just reduce the amount of salt in this recipe if they are already seasoned.

DESSERT

Sugar cooked down to a caramel, then blended with cream and a touch of sea salt makes a luscious sauce to drizzle over waffles. If you like, add sliced peaches and toasted pecans on top along with the whipped cream.

Waffles with Salted Caramel Sauce

For the Salted Caramel Sauce

1 cup (8 fl oz/250 ml) heavy cream

1 cup (8 oz/250 g) sugar

1 teaspoon pure vanilla extract

Dash of *fleur de sel* or sea salt

Classic Waffle Batter (page 91), made with ¼ cup (2 oz/60 g) sugar

Whipped Cream (page 77)

MAKES 4-8 WAFFLES

Egg Waffle Variation

Preheat an egg waffle pan according to the manufacturer's instructions. Ladle the batter into one side of the pan, using ¾ cup (6 fl oz/180 ml) batter per waffle. Immediately place the other side of the pan on top, and flip the pan over. Flip the pan again halfway through the cooking time (see page 11).

To make the salted caramel sauce, in a small saucepan over medium-low heat, warm the cream until bubbles form around the sides; do not boil. Keep warm. Place the sugar and ½ cup (4 fl oz/125 ml) water in another small saucepan. Heat to medium and cook, stirring, until the sugar dissolves. Without stirring, let the syrup slowly boil, brushing any sugar from the walls of the pan with a wet pastry brush. Cook until the syrup turns light brown, 10–15 minutes, watching carefully; once it starts to change color, it can burn easily.

Remove the caramel from the heat. While the cream is still hot (to avoid splattering), pour it into the caramel while whisking constantly. Return the mixture to low heat and cook until smooth, 2–3 minutes. Remove from the heat and add the vanilla and sea salt to taste. (The salted caramel can be made up to 2 weeks ahead. Cover tightly and refrigerate, then reheat gently to serve.)

Preheat a waffle maker (see page 11). Prepare the batter according to the directions on page 91, using ¼ cup sugar.

Ladle the batter into the waffle maker, using ½–¾ cup (4–6 fl oz/125–180 ml) batter per batch. Spread the batter so that it almost reaches the edges of the waffle maker. Cook until the waffles are crisp and browned, 3–4 minutes.

Using a spatula, remove the waffles from the waffle maker and serve right away, or place on a baking sheet in a single layer in a 200°F (95°C) oven for up to 20 minutes before serving. Top with the whipped cream and drizzle with salted caramel sauce.

Hidden inside these waffles are pockets of crunchy nuts and gooey melted white chocolate and butterscotch. They are perfect simply topped with whipped cream, but you could add a scoop of ice cream or a drizzle of Chocolate Syrup (page 93).

White Chocolate–Butterscotch Waffles with Almonds

Classic Waffle Batter (page 91), made with ¼ cup (2 oz/60 g) sugar

2 oz (60 g) white chocolate, chopped into pieces (see Note)

⅓ cup (2 oz/60 g) butterscotch chips

¼ cup (1½ oz/45 g) slivered or finely chopped almonds

Whipped Cream (page 77; optional)

MAKES 4–8 WAFFLES

Preheat a waffle maker (see page 11). Prepare the batter according to the directions on page 91, using ¼ cup sugar.

Ladle the batter into the waffle maker, using ½–¾ cup (4–6 fl oz/ 125–180 ml) batter per batch. Spread the batter so that it almost reaches the edges of the waffle maker. Quickly sprinkle the waffles with 1–2 teaspoons white chocolate pieces, 2–3 teaspoons butterscotch chips, and 1–2 teaspoons almonds, then close the lid. Cook until the waffles are crisp and browned, 3–4 minutes. Wipe the waffle maker clean between batches, in case there is any burned chocolate or butterscotch remaining.

Using a spatula, remove the waffles from the waffle maker and serve right away, or place on a baking sheet in a single layer in a 200°F (95°C) oven for up to 20 minutes before serving. Top with whipped cream, if using.

NOTE: When purchasing white chocolate, look for brands with a high cocoa butter content. It's better to use a chopped white chocolate bar than white chocolate chips, because many chips are very low in cocoa butter or lack it completely.

Featuring fresh pineapple and raw sugar, these are like the waffle version of a tiki cocktail. You can also sprinkle them with brown sugar, which has a similar molasses flavor. Serve with Salted Caramel Sauce (page 73), if you like.

Pineapple Waffles with Raw Sugar

Classic Waffle Batter (page 91), made with ¼ cup (2 oz/60 g) granulated sugar

1 cup (6 oz/185 g) chopped fresh pineapple (see Note)

About ⅓ cup (3 oz/90 g) raw or turbinado sugar

MAKES 4–8 WAFFLES

Egg Waffle Variation

Preheat an egg waffle pan according to the manufacturer's instructions. Ladle the batter into one side of the pan, using ¾ cup (6 fl oz/180 ml) batter per waffle. Immediately place the other side of the pan on top, and flip the pan over. Flip the pan again halfway through the cooking time (see page 11).

Preheat a waffle maker (see page 11). Prepare the batter according to the directions on page 91, using ¼ cup granulated sugar. Gently stir in the chopped pineapple.

Ladle the batter into the waffle maker, using ½–¾ cup (4–6 fl oz/125–180 ml) batter per batch. Spread the batter so that it almost reaches the edges of the waffle maker, and distribute the pineapple pieces around each waffle. Sprinkle each waffle with 2–3 teaspoons of the raw sugar, depending on the size of the waffle. Cook until the waffles are crisp and browned, 3–4 minutes.

Using a spatula, remove the waffles from the waffle maker and serve right away, or place on a baking sheet in a single layer in a 200°F (95°C) oven for up to 20 minutes before serving.

NOTE: To chop a fresh pineapple, first cut off the base and top. Place the pineapple upright on a cutting board and remove the skin in long, downward slices. Quarter the fruit lengthwise, then remove the core from each piece. Chop the fruit into ¼-inch (6-mm) dice.

Studded with chocolate, these waffles are perfect with just a dollop of whipped cream, but it never hurts to add extras like Strawberry Sauce (page 85). These waffles are also an ideal choice for the Ice-Cream Waffle Sandwiches (page 87).

Chocolate Chip Waffles with Whipped Cream

For the Whipped Cream

1 cup (8 fl oz/250 ml) heavy cream

2 tablespoons granulated sugar

¼ teaspoon pure vanilla extract

Classic Waffle Batter (page 91), made with ¼ cup (2 oz/60 g) granulated sugar

About 1½ cups (9 oz/280 g) chocolate chips, either milk or semisweet (see Note), plus more for serving

Confectioners' sugar for serving

MAKES 4–8 WAFFLES

To make the whipped cream, in the bowl of a stand mixer using the whisk attachment, whip the cream on medium-high speed until soft peaks form, about 3 minutes. Add the granulated sugar and vanilla and whip until firmer peaks form, 1–2 minutes.

Preheat a waffle maker (see page 11). Prepare the batter according to the directions on page 91, using ¼ cup granulated sugar.

Ladle the batter into the waffle maker, using ½–¾ cup (4–6 fl oz/ 125–180 ml) batter per batch. Spread the batter so that it almost reaches the edges of the waffle maker. Quickly sprinkle 3–4 tablespoons chocolate chips over the top, then close the lid. Cook until the waffles are crisp and browned, 3–4 minutes. Wipe the waffle maker clean between batches, in case there are any burned chocolate chips.

Using a spatula, remove the waffles from the waffle maker and serve right away, or place on a baking sheet in a single layer in a 200°F (95°C) oven for up to 20 minutes before serving. Dust with confectioners' sugar and top with a dollop of whipped cream. Garnish each waffle with a few chocolate chips.

NOTE: Because these waffles aren't overly sweet, you may want to use only milk chocolate chips or a mixture of milk chocolate and semisweet chocolate chips.

In this recipe, chocolate waffles are paired with luscious peanut butter cream. Slice the waffles into sticks for dipping, or you can cut out waffle squares and sandwich with the cream, ala whoopie pies.

Chocolate Waffle Bites with Peanut Butter Cream

For the Peanut Butter Cream

⅓ cup (3½ oz/105 g) creamy peanut butter (see Note)

¼ cup (2 fl oz/60 ml) whole milk

3 tablespoons sugar

1 cup (8 fl oz/250 ml) heavy cream

Chocolate Waffle Batter (page 93)

MAKES 4–8 WAFFLES

Egg Waffle Variation

Preheat an egg waffle pan according to the manufacturer's instructions. Ladle the batter into one side of the pan, using ¾ cup (6 fl oz/180 ml) batter per waffle. Immediately place the other side of the pan on top, and flip the pan over. Flip the pan again halfway through the cooking time (see page 11).

To make the peanut butter cream, in a small, heavy saucepan over medium-low heat, cook the peanut butter, milk, and sugar, whisking constantly, until the mixture is just smooth, 1–2 minutes. Do not overcook. Remove from the heat and place in a stainless steel or glass bowl and cool to lukewarm, 5–10 minutes.

In the bowl of a stand mixer, using the whisk attachment, whip the cream on medium-high speed until peaks form, 4–5 minutes. Gently fold in the peanut butter mixture by hand. (The peanut butter cream can be made up to 3 hours ahead. Cover tightly and refrigerate, and whisk gently before serving.) Place the peanut butter cream in a serving bowl or in ramekins.

Preheat a waffle-stick or waffle maker (see page 11) to medium-high. Prepare the batter according to the directions on page 93.

Ladle the batter into the waffle maker, using ½–¾ cup (4–6 fl oz/ 125–180 ml) batter per batch. Spread the batter so that it almost reaches the edges of the waffle maker. Cook until the waffles are crisp, 3–4 minutes.

Using a spatula, remove the waffles from the waffle-stick or waffle maker. If using a waffle maker, place the waffles on cooling racks and allow to stand for 1 minute to crisp. Using a bread knife, slice the waffles into sticks 1 inch (2.5 cm) wide, and then in half, making large bite-sized pieces. Serve with the peanut butter cream for dipping.

NOTE: For best results, use salted but unsweetened peanut butter.

Adding cooked rice to the batter gives the waffles a crisp texture, while the coconut and mangoes suggest the flavors of a Thai dessert. Whipped cream lightly flavored with lime is the perfect topping.

Coconut-Rice Waffles with Mangoes and Lime Cream

For the Lime Cream

1 cup (8 fl oz/250 ml) heavy cream

1/2 cup (4 oz/125 g) sour cream or crème fraîche

1/4 cup (1 oz/30 g) confectioners' sugar, plus more as needed

2 teaspoons finely grated lime zest

2 teaspoons fresh lime juice

2 large eggs

1 can (13.5 fl oz/400 ml) coconut milk, well-shaken before opening

1/4 cup (2 fl oz/60 ml) canola oil or coconut oil

1 teaspoon pure vanilla extract

1 cup (5 oz/155 g) all-purpose flour

1/4 cup (2 oz/60 g) granulated sugar

1 tablespoon baking powder

1/4 teaspoon salt

1 cup (5 oz/155 g) cooked white rice (see Note)

1/2 cup (2 oz/60 g) dried unsweetened coconut

2–3 large ripe mangoes, sliced

MAKES 4-8 WAFFLES

To make the lime cream, in the bowl of a stand mixer using the whisk attachment, whip the cream and sour cream on medium-high speed until soft peaks form, about 3 minutes. Add the 1/4 cup confectioners' sugar, lime zest, and lime juice and whisk until just set, 1–2 minutes. Taste and add more confectioners' sugar if you like. (The lime cream can be made 3 hours ahead; cover and refrigerate.)

Preheat a waffle maker (see page 11).

In a medium bowl, whisk the eggs, coconut milk, oil, and vanilla.

In a large bowl, mix together the flour, granulated sugar, baking powder, and salt. Stir in the rice and coconut. Make a well in the center of the dry ingredients, then pour in the egg mixture. Whisk until mostly smooth, with just a few lumps.

Ladle the batter into the waffle maker, using 1/2–3/4 cup (4–6 fl oz/ 125–180 ml) batter per batch. Spread the batter so that it almost reaches the edges of the waffle maker. Cook until the waffles are crisp, 3–4 minutes.

Using a spatula, remove the waffles from the waffle maker and serve right away, or place on a baking sheet in a single layer in a 200°F (95°C) oven for up to 20 minutes before serving. Top with the mango slices and a dollop of the lime cream.

NOTE: If you don't have cooked rice, substitute 1/2 cup (2 1/2 oz/75 g) all-purpose flour.

Whole-wheat, honey, and cinnamon combined with melted marshmallows and chocolate bring back campfire memories. Just as you would outdoors, cook the marshmallows carefully and don't place them too close to the flame.

Waffle S'mores

2 large eggs

1½ cups (12 fl oz/375 ml) whole milk

½ cup (4 oz/125 g) unsalted butter, melted, or ½ cup (4 fl oz/125 ml) canola oil

2 tablespoons honey

¾ cup (4 oz/125 g) all-purpose flour

¾ cup (4 oz/125 g) whole-wheat flour

3 tablespoons firmly packed golden brown sugar

1 tablespoon baking powder

½ teaspoon cinnamon

¼ teaspoon salt

1 tablespoon granulated sugar mixed with 1 teaspoon cinnamon

½ cup (3 oz/90 g) chocolate chips, semisweet, milk, or a combination

2 cups (3½ oz/105 g) mini marshmallows

MAKES 4–8 WAFFLES

Preheat a waffle maker (see page 11). Preheat the oven to broil, and arrange a rack 6–8 inches (15–20 cm) from the broiler. Line a baking sheet with foil.

In a medium bowl, whisk together the eggs, milk, butter, and honey.

In a large bowl, mix together the all-purpose flour, whole-wheat flour, brown sugar, baking powder, cinnamon, and salt. Make a well in the center of the dry ingredients, then pour in the egg mixture. Whisk until mostly smooth, with just a few lumps.

Ladle the batter into the waffle maker, using ½–¾ cup (4–6 fl oz/ 125–180 ml) batter per batch. Spread the batter so that it almost reaches the edges of the waffle maker. Cook until the waffles are crisp and browned, 3–4 minutes.

Using a spatula, remove the waffles from the waffle maker. Place the waffles on the prepared baking sheet and sprinkle with the cinnamon sugar. (You can make the waffles to this point up to 4 hours ahead. Cool completely; then stack, wrap tightly, and refrigerate.)

It's a good idea to do one test waffle to see how quickly your broiler works. Divide the chocolate chips and mini marshmallows among the waffles. (If you used a Belgian waffle maker, you can place the marshmallows and chocolate chips inside the holes in a tic-tac-toe pattern.) Place the baking sheet on the rack and keep the oven door ajar. Watch and broil until the marshmallows are lightly browned, 1–2 minutes. Cut the waffles into quarters and serve right away.

With their short summer season, sweet-tart raspberries deserve to star in their own dessert waffle. Here they pair with an easy and fresh sauce that tastes a little like lemon curd, especially when you add whipped cream.

Raspberry Waffles with Lemon Sauce

For the Lemon Sauce

2 tablespoons cornstarch

²/₃ cup (5 oz/155 g) sugar

4 teaspoons finely grated lemon zest

¼ cup (2 fl oz/60 ml) fresh lemon juice

2 tablespoons unsalted butter, chopped into pieces

Pinch of salt

Classic Waffle Batter (page 91), made with ⅓ cup (3 oz/90 g) sugar

1 cup (4 oz/125 g) fresh raspberries

Whipped Cream (page 77; optional)

MAKES 8 WAFFLES

To make the lemon sauce, in a small bowl, combine the cornstarch and ½ cup (4 fl oz/125 ml) water.

Place 1½ cups (12 fl oz/375 ml) water in a small saucepan with the sugar. Cook over medium heat, stirring, until the sugar melts and the mixture is clear, about 3 minutes. Add the cornstarch mixture, then simmer until it thickens, 2–3 minutes. Remove from the heat and stir in the lemon zest, lemon juice, butter, and salt. Keep warm.

Preheat a waffle maker (see page 11). Prepare the batter according to the directions on page 91, using ⅓ cup (3 oz/90 g) sugar. Gently stir in the raspberries.

Ladle the batter into the waffle maker, using ½–¾ cup (4–6 fl oz/ 125–180 ml) batter per batch. Spread the batter so that it almost reaches the edges of the waffle maker, and evenly distribute the raspberries. Cook until the waffles are crisp and browned, 3–4 minutes.

Using a spatula, remove the waffles from the waffle maker and serve right away, or place on a baking sheet in a single layer in a 200°F (95°C) oven for up to 20 minutes before serving. Drizzle with the lemon sauce and top with the whipped cream, if using.

Chocolate waffles, studded with extra chocolate chips, get a drizzle of fresh strawberry sauce in this pretty dessert. Try the sauce on its own with ice cream or with other waffles such as Lemon–Poppy Seed (page 28).

Double-Chocolate Waffles with Strawberry Sauce

For the Strawberry Sauce

2 pints (1 lb/500 g) fresh strawberries, stemmed, cored, and sliced

4–5 tablespoons (2–2½ oz/ 60–70 g) sugar

Chocolate Waffle Batter (page 93)

1 cup (6 oz/185 g) semisweet chocolate chips

Whipped Cream (page 77) or ice cream (optional)

MAKES 4-8 WAFFLES

To make the strawberry sauce, place the strawberries and sugar in a saucepan and stir well. Cook over medium heat, stirring, until the sugar melts, then cover and cook on a low simmer until the strawberries soften and release their liquid, about 5 minutes. Scrape the mixture into a blender or food processor, and blend until smooth. Taste and add more sugar if you like. (The sauce keeps for up to 1 week. Cover tightly and refrigerate, and reheat gently to serve.)

Preheat a waffle maker (see page 11) to medium-high. Prepare the batter according to the directions on page 93.

Ladle the batter into the waffle maker, using ½–¾ cup (4–6 fl oz/ 125–180 ml) batter per batch. Spread the batter so that it almost reaches the edges of the waffle maker. Sprinkle evenly with chocolate chips, then close the lid and cook until the waffles are crisp and browned, 3–4 minutes. Wipe the waffle maker clean between batches, in case there is any burned chocolate.

Using a spatula, remove the waffles from the waffle maker and serve right away, or place on a baking sheet in a single layer in a 200°F (95°C) oven for up to 20 minutes before serving. Top with the strawberry sauce and the whipped cream, if using.

Using waffles in ice-cream sandwiches conjures up memories of waffle cones, and there are endless possibilities for flavor combinations. Freeze the sandwiches briefly to prevent melting, but not so long that the waffles lose their crispiness.

Ice-Cream Waffle Sandwiches

Batter for Vanilla Bean Belgian Waffles (page 19),

About 1 quart (18 oz/560 g) ice cream of your choice

½–1 cup (5½–11 oz/170–345 g) Chocolate Syrup (page 93) or Salted Caramel Sauce (page 73) (optional)

MAKES 6–12 SANDWICHES

Batter Variation
You can also make this recipe with the batter for Chocolate Chip Waffles (page 77), Gingerbread Waffles (page 36), White Chocolate–Butterscotch Waffles (page 74), or Chocolate Waffles (page 93).

Preheat a waffle maker (see page 11). Prepare the batter according to the directions on page 19.

Ladle the batter into the waffle maker, using ½–¾ cup (4–6 fl oz/ 125–180 ml) batter per batch. Spread the batter so that it almost reaches the edges of the waffle maker. Cook until the waffles are crisp and browned, 3–4 minutes.

Using a spatula, remove the waffles from the waffle maker. Place on racks and allow to cool completely.

Allow the ice cream to soften slightly at room temperature for about 10 minutes.

Separate the waffles into quarters or halves, depending on their size. Scoop the ice cream onto half of the pieces, in 4 small half-scoops, and spread to fit over the waffle, if desired, or fill in empty spaces with a little ice cream. If using syrup or sauce, drizzle 1–2 tablespoons on top of the ice cream in each sandwich. Top with the other waffle, then wrap in plastic wrap and return to the freezer for 20–60 minutes.

Slice waffle sandwiches in half on the diagonal and serve right away.

Belgian or chocolate waffles make a crunchy, buttery accent to a classic banana split. This is a good way to use any homemade ones you may have in your freezer; just toast frozen waffles until crisp.

Waffle Banana Splits

2–4 large cooked Vanilla Bean Belgian Waffles (page 19)

4–6 bananas, halved lengthwise and widthwise

4 scoops vanilla ice cream

4 scoops strawberry ice cream

Whipped Cream (page 77)

Chocolate Syrup (page 93), lightly warmed

Salted Caramel Sauce (page 73) or purchased caramel or butterscotch sauce, lightly warmed (optional)

¼ cup (1½ oz/45 g) chopped almonds

4 maraschino cherries

MAKES 4 SERVINGS

Batter Variation
You can also make this recipe with the batter for Chocolate Chip Waffles (page 77), Gingerbread Waffles (page 36), White Chocolate–Butterscotch Waffles (page 74), or Chocolate Waffles (page 93).

Toast the waffles lightly in a toaster oven or on a baking sheet in a 350°F (180°C) oven until crisp, 5–10 minutes.

Cut the waffles in half on the diagonal and place in the bottom of ice cream bowls or banana-split dishes. Place the banana pieces on top of the waffle pieces, and top with the scoops of ice cream, whipped cream, chocolate syrup, salted caramel sauce, if using, and almonds. Top each with a cherry. Serve right away.

basic recipes

Classic Waffle Batter

This versatile batter works with any number of flavorings, a mixture of flours, and diverse toppings. For dessert waffles, increase the amount of sugar by at least 1 tablespoon.

2 large eggs

1½ cups (12 fl oz/375 ml) whole milk

½ cup (4 oz/125 g) unsalted butter, melted, or ½ cup (4 fl oz/125 ml) canola oil

1 teaspoon pure vanilla extract

1½ cups (7½ oz/235 g) all-purpose flour

3 tablespoons sugar

1 tablespoon baking powder

¼ teaspoon salt

In a medium bowl, whisk together the eggs, milk, butter, and vanilla.

In a large bowl, mix together the flour, sugar, baking powder, and salt. Make a well in the center of the dry ingredients, then pour in the egg mixture. Whisk until mostly smooth, with just a few lumps.

MAKES 4–8 WAFFLES

Belgian Waffle Batter

This is a basic version of the batter for Vanilla Bean Belgian Waffles (page 19). The main difference between this batter and the Classic Waffle Batter (above) is that the egg whites are whipped separately, which adds a little more volume and lightness.

3 large eggs, separated

1½ cups (12 fl oz/375 ml) whole milk

½ cup (4 oz/125 g) unsalted butter, melted

1½ teaspoons pure vanilla extract

1¾ cups (9 oz/280 g) all-purpose flour

2 teaspoons baking powder

¼ teaspoon salt

3 tablespoons sugar

In a medium bowl, mix together the egg yolks, milk, butter, and vanilla.

In a large bowl, mix together the flour, baking powder, and salt.

In the bowl of a stand mixer using the whisk attachment, whip the egg whites on medium-high speed until soft peaks form, about 3 minutes. Add the sugar and whip until firm peaks form, 2–3 minutes.

Make a well in the center of the dry ingredients, and pour in the milk mixture, stirring until just combined. Gently fold in the egg whites.

MAKES 6–10 WAFFLES

Buttermilk Waffle Batter

The addition of buttermilk means these waffles are not too sweet, making this a great all-purpose recipe. If you don't have buttermilk, you can substitute whole milk slightly curdled with vinegar (see Note).

2 large eggs

1½ cups (12 fl oz/375 ml) buttermilk (see Note), plus more as needed

½ cup (4 oz/125 g) unsalted butter, melted, or ½ cup (4 fl oz/125 ml) canola oil

1½ cups (7½ oz/235 g) all-purpose flour

2 tablespoons sugar

2 teaspoons baking powder

1 teaspoon baking soda

¼ teaspoon salt

In a medium bowl, whisk together the eggs, buttermilk, and butter.

In a large bowl, mix the flour, sugar, baking powder, baking soda, and salt. Make a well in the center of the dry ingredients, then pour in the egg mixture. Whisk until mostly smooth, with just a few lumps. If the batter seems like it is too thick, stir in another 1–2 tablespoons buttermilk.

Note: For the buttermilk, you can substitute 1½ cups (12 fl oz/375 ml) whole milk combined with 1½ tablespoons distilled or white wine vinegar; let sit 10 minutes to sour and slightly curdle the milk.

MAKES 4–8 WAFFLES

Cornmeal Waffle Batter

This version of the Buttermilk Waffle Batter (page 91) is designed for Cornmeal-Bacon Waffles with Thyme-Infused Syrup (page 44) and Cornmeal Waffles with Tomato Chutney (page 56). For a more basic breakfast waffle, increase the sugar to 2 tablespoons and omit the pepper.

2 large eggs

1½ cups (12 fl oz/375 ml) buttermilk (see Note above), plus more as needed

½ cup (4 oz/125 g) unsalted butter, melted, or ½ cup (4 fl oz/125 ml) canola oil

¾ cup (4 oz/125 g) cornmeal

¾ cup (4 oz/125 g) all-purpose flour

4 teaspoons sugar

2 teaspoons baking powder

1 teaspoon baking soda

¾ teaspoon salt

¼ teaspoon black pepper (optional)

In a medium bowl, whisk together the eggs, buttermilk, and butter.

In a large bowl, mix together the cornmeal, flour, sugar, baking powder, baking soda, salt, and pepper, if using. Make a well in the center of the dry ingredients, then pour in the egg mixture. Whisk until mostly smooth, with just a few lumps. If the batter is too thick, stir in another 1–2 tablespoons buttermilk.

MAKES 4–8 WAFFLES

Multigrain Waffle Batter

This recipe is perfect for savory Multigrain Waffles with Avocado and Tomato-Almond Pesto (page 61), and it also works with sweet toppings for breakfast. You can mix and match the grains that you use, depending on what's in your cupboard.

2 large eggs

1½ cups (12 fl oz/375 ml) whole milk

½ cup (4 oz/125 g) unsalted butter, melted, or ½ cup (4 fl oz/125 ml) canola oil

½ cup (2½ oz/75 g) all-purpose flour

¼ cup (1½ oz/45 g) whole-wheat flour

¼ cup (1½ oz/45 g) buckwheat flour

¼ cup (1½ oz/45 g) cornmeal

¼ cup (¾ oz/20 g) rolled oats

2 tablespoons sugar

1 tablespoon baking powder

¼ teaspoon salt

In a medium bowl, whisk together the eggs, milk, and butter.

In a large bowl, mix together the all-purpose flour, whole-wheat flour, buckwheat flour, cornmeal, oats, sugar, baking powder, and salt. Make a well in the center of the dry ingredients, then pour in the egg mixture. Whisk until mostly smooth, with just a few lumps.

MAKES 4–8 WAFFLES

Overnight Sourdough Waffle Batter

Make a batch of these lacy waffles at breakfast, then use leftover batter later in Sourdough Waffle BLTs (page 55). Though not technically sourdough, these raised waffles have a sour tang and are inspired by cookbook author Marion Cunningham's famous recipe.

1 package (2½ teaspoons) active dry yeast

½ cup (4 fl oz/125 ml) water warmed to 110°F (43°C)

2 cups (10 oz/315 g) all-purpose flour

1½ cups (12 fl oz/375 ml) warm buttermilk or whole milk

½ cup (4 oz/125 g) unsalted butter, melted, or ½ cup (4 fl oz/125 ml) canola oil

1 tablespoon sugar

½ teaspoon salt

2 large eggs

½ teaspoon baking soda

In a small bowl or glass measuring cup, combine the yeast with the water. Let stand until bubbly, about 10 minutes. In a large bowl, combine the flour, buttermilk, butter, sugar, and salt, and mix with the yeast until blended. Cover with plastic wrap or a towel and let stand in a warm part of the kitchen overnight.

In the morning, stir in the eggs and baking soda. (The batter will hold for 2–3 days. Cover tightly and refrigerate.)

MAKES 6-10 WAFFLES

Chocolate Waffle Batter

These are definitely dessert waffles, yet they don't taste too sweet. Try them in the Ice-Cream Waffle Sandwiches (page 87) or the Double Chocolate Waffles with Strawberry Sauce (page 85).

½ cup (3 oz/90 g) semisweet chocolate chips or bittersweet chocolate

4 tablespoons (2 oz/60 g) unsalted butter

2 large eggs

1½ cups (12 fl oz/375 ml) whole milk

2 teaspoons pure vanilla extract

1¾ cups (9 oz/280 g) all-purpose flour

1 cup (8 oz/250 g) sugar

¼ cup (¾ oz/20 g) unsweetened cocoa powder

1 tablespoon baking powder

½ teaspoon salt

Place the chocolate chips and butter in a double boiler and heat until melted, about 5 minutes. Whisk to incorporate. Let cool slightly. In a medium bowl, whisk together the eggs, milk, and vanilla. Slowly whisk in the chocolate mixture to incorporate.

In a large bowl, mix together the flour, sugar, cocoa powder, baking powder, and salt. Make a well in the center of the dry ingredients, then pour in the egg mixture. Whisk until mostly smooth, with just a few lumps.

MAKES 4-8 WAFFLES

Chocolate Syrup

This sauce couldn't be easier to make. Use it drizzled over the Waffle Banana Splits (page 88) or in the Ice-Cream Waffle Sandwiches (page 87), or just stir it into milk for hot chocolate.

1 cup (8 oz/250 g) sugar

¼ cup (2½ oz/75 g) light corn syrup

¾ cup (2½ oz/75 g) unsweetened cocoa powder

Pinch of salt

2 teaspoons pure vanilla extract

Combine the sugar and corn syrup with 1 cup (8 fl oz/250 ml) water in a small saucepan. Stir over medium heat until the sugar dissolves, then mix in the cocoa powder and salt. Simmer until smooth, 3 minutes, stirring occasionally. Add the vanilla and let cool. (The syrup will keep for up to 3 weeks. Cover and refrigerate.)

MAKES ABOUT 1 CUP (11 OZ/345 G)

index

weldonowen

415 Jackson Street, Suite 200, San Francisco, CA 94111
Telephone: 415 291 0100 Fax: 415 291 8841
www.weldonowen.com

Weldon Owen is a division of
BONNIER

WELDON OWEN, INC.

CEO and President Terry Newell
VP, Sales and Marketing Amy Kaneko
Director of Finance Mark Perrigo

VP and Publisher Hannah Rahill
Executive Editor Jennifer Newens
Editor Donita Boles
Assistant Editor Becky Duffett

Creative Director Emma Boys
Art Director Alexandra Zeigler

Production Director Chris Hemesath
Production Manager Michelle Duggan
Color Manager Teri Bell

Photographer Erin Kunkel
Food Stylist Kevin Crafts
Prop Stylist Ethel Brennan

WAFFLES

Conceived and produced by Weldon Owen, Inc.
Copyright © 2011 Weldon Owen, Inc.

Printed and bound by 1010 Printing, Ltd. in China

First printed in 2011
10 9 8 7 6 5

Library of Congress Control Number:
2011930623

ISBN-13: 978-1-61628-205-9
ISBN-10: 1-61628-205-3

ACKNOWLEDGMENTS

Weldon Owen wishes to thank the following people for their generous support
in producing this book: David Bornfriend, Ken DellaPenta, Jennifer Hale,
Rachel Lopez Metzger, Lesli J. Neilson, Karen Seriguchi, Abby Stolfo, and Tracy White Taylor.
The author wishes to thank Jenna Meyer for her help in the kitchen.